The heart-traveller

7

Sri Chinmoy

Eternity's Breath

Aphorisms and essays

Ganapati Press

© 2023 SRI CHINMOY CENTRE

ISBN 978-1-911319-51-1

FIRST EDITION WENT TO PRESS ON 27 August 2023

Eternity's Breath

I — Aphorisms

1. *Aum*

AUM is the soundless sound. It is the vibration of the Supreme. It is called the Seed-Sound of the Universe, for with this sound, the Supreme set into motion the first vibration of His creation. The teeming universe is sustained perpetually by the creative vibration of the Divine AUM.

The syllable AUM is indivisible, but each portion of it represents a different aspect of the Supreme. The Sanskrit A represents and embodies the Consciousness of the Creator, Brahma; the Sanskrit U, the Preserver, Vishnu; the Sanskrit M, the Transformer, Shiva. Taken together, AUM is the spontaneous cosmic rhythm with which God embraces the universe.

The universal AUM, put forth by the Supreme, is an infinite Ocean. The individual AUM, chanted by man, is a drop in that Ocean. It cannot be separated from the Ocean but nevertheless even the tiniest drop can claim the Ocean as its very own. Chanting AUM, man touches and calls forth the cosmic vibration of the Supreme Sound. When one can hear the Soundless Sound within oneself, when one can identify oneself with it, when one can live within the AUM, one can be freed from the fetters of ignorance and realise the Supreme within and without.

The unknown embraces ignorance with its self-limitation. The unknowable embraces AUM with His absolute Self-revelation.

Without birth is the Supreme; without birth is AUM. Without end is the Supreme; without end is AUM. Immortality is AUM's universal Identity.

When we are in ignorance, AUM feeds us, for AUM is God. When we are in Knowledge, AUM still feeds us. When we are beyond both ignorance and Knowledge, AUM continues to feed us, for it is the nectar which gives life to creation, born and unborn.

2. Creation and evolution

The Self-Division of the Supreme proclaims the birth of creation.

Creation is the descent of Consciousness. Creation is a never-tiring march which marks the beginning of an inner and outer development.

What is evolution, if not the veiled determination of an apparent unconsciousness seeking conscious formation and growth?

Nature is the evolving phenomenon, while Consciousness is its guide in evolution. At each stage, nature transcends the limits of its own species and presses forward to new conquests.

The real development and progress of life must always sit at the feet of the Dynamic Divine and not at the feet of the Static Divine.

In the march of evolution, each period has a demand of its own. Each incarnation of God fulfils that very demand.

Our self-division can play, at most, with the divided selves of the Supreme and never with the Supreme's inseparable Oneness.

3. Love: *sacrifice*

Fulfilment is nothing but voluntary sacrifice.

Where your sacrifice is, there will as well be your delight.

Sacrifice is fulfilment attained. Surrender is delight obtained. Love is union manifested.

Love is precious. Surrender is more precious. Union is still more precious.

Self-giving alone has free access to Joy everlasting.

It has been delightfully claimed that: "Love in France is a comedy; in England a tragedy; in Italy an opera seria; and in Germany a melodrama." In the true Indian tradition love has always been a self-offering and a self-fulfilment.

4. Love: human and divine

Divine Love is a flowering of delight and self-giving. Human love is the gambol of sufferings and limitations.

Love is a bird. When we encage it, we call it human love. When we allow love to fly in the all-pervading Consciousness, we call it Divine Love.

Ordinary human love with its fears, accusations, misunderstandings, jealousies and quarrels is a fire clouding its own brightness by a pall of smoke. The same human love, arising from the meeting of two souls, is a pure and radiant flame. Instead of smoke, it emits the rays of self-surrender, sacrifice, selflessness, joy and fulfilment.

Human love is often the terrible attraction of bodies and nerves; Divine Love is the ever-blossoming affinity of souls.

Divine Love is detachment; human love is attachment. Detachment is real satisfaction. Attachment is quenchless thirst.

Ascending love, arising from the soul's joy, is

the smile of God. Descending love, carrying with it the passion of the senses, is the kiss of Death.

Human love is usually self-embracing and self-persistent. Divine Love is all-embracing and self-existent.

Love can be as brittle as glass or as strong as Eternity, depending upon whether it is founded in the vital or in the Soul.

Our higher emotions, taken away from their human objects and offered to God, are turned into Divine Nectar by His magic. Our lower emotions, if not transmuted and transformed, are turned into poison by our own hand.

Disappointment skilfully dogs vital love. Satisfaction divinely consummates psychic love.

When our vital wants to see something, it has to look through self-love. When our Psychic Being wants to see something, it sees through self-giving.

Human love says to Divine Love: "I can't tolerate you." Divine Love says to human love: "Well, that is no reason for me to leave you."

5. Love: attachment and detachment

If human affection is not always reliable, it is also not always harmful. Foolish is he who thinks that affection should be turned into indifference in order that God might come to him. Alas, he has yet to learn that God is All-Affection.

Affection and attachment need not always go together. An entire rejection of all relations can never be the promising sign of progress towards Realisation.

Controlled desire is good. Better is non-attachment. Best is it to feel oneself removed from the snare of nature. Suppression is as hostile and undeserving as attachment. It is our non-attachment that is the only master of nature.

Desires and hungers have one common enemy: detachment.

Detachment and not possession should be the bridge between you and the object of your love.

Spiritual detachment intensifies the seeking of our hearts, purifies the vibrations of our bodies, transforms the ignorance of our consciousness into knowledge.

Granted, loneliness is a kind of spiritual disease. But human association can never be its lasting medicine. The only permanent cure for it is Inner Experience.

6. *Love: a divine power*

> Blue eyes say: "Love me or I die."
> Black eyes say: "Love me or I kill thee."
>
> – Spanish proverb

Red-angered eyes say: "Whether thou lovest me or not, I have come to kill thee." But soul-illumined eyes say: "I see God in thee and love thee whether thou killest me or not."

No doubt, life precedes love. But if love does not follow life faithfully, life is no better than death.

Love in the process of its manifestation is conscious truth enjoying itself.

If you ever dare to fight against hatred, then there is but one weapon: Love.

When I love a man, I live within his ever-blossoming heart. When I hate a man, he lives within my ever-torturing vital.

Love has a power of its own. It can be used to see and feel both the lowest and the highest.

The noblest love of man constitutes his purest vision of God.

Love is always expensive, whether heavenly or earthly.

Like death, man's love is capable of levelling all ranks.

To have no love for others is in no way a step towards God-Realisation. On the contrary, fellow-feeling helps one considerably to live in the Divine Consciousness.

Vital love lacking in purity is not only a stumbling-block but a dangerous limitation of consciousness that prevents our nature from turning towards the Divine fully and unreservedly.

Marriage is at the mercy of love. At times love allows itself to be caught by marriage; at times it does not.

Ascending love makes friends with the Everlasting. Descending love makes friends with the fleeting breath of death.

> 'Tis better to have loved and lost,
> Than never to have loved at all.
>
> – Tennyson

But can true love ever be lost? True love enlarges the giver and brings him closer to God, even if he loses the object of his love.

7. Devotion

Devotion is the complete submission of the individual will to the Will Divine. Devotion is adoration. Adoration is the spontaneous delight that springs from the heart. Who can be the object of our adoration? God. How can we adore Him? Through our self-surrender.

Man loves. He expects love in return. A devotee loves. But he loves human beings for the sake of his sweet Lord who abides in all. His love breathes in humility, spontaneous joy and selfless service.

Devotion is the feminine aspect of love. It is sweet, energising and complete. Sri Aurobindo says, "After I knew that God was a woman, I learned something from far-off about love; but it was only when I became a woman and served my Master and Paramour that I knew love utterly."

A devotee sees a circle which is God. He enters into it with his soul's cry. He then silently comes and stands at the centre of the circle and grows into a tree of ecstasy.

A child does not care to know what his mother

is. He just wants his mother's constant presence of love before him. Similar is the devotee's feeling for his Lord. Many come forward to help him in his life's journey. But he cares not for their help. God's Grace is his sole help and refuge. The tortures of hell are too weak to torment him while he is there with his Lord. His life in hell is a life of perfect bliss. His sufferings and tribulations in Heaven know no bounds if he is there without his Lord beside him.

Devotion is a soul-stirring emotion. It dynamically permeates the entire consciousness of the devotee. Devotion is action. This action is always inspired by the devotee's inner being.

Devotion brings in renunciation. True renunciation is never a life of isolation. Renunciation is an utter distaste for the animal life of the flesh. It is also a total absence of the ego. A life of true renunciation is a life that lives in the world but does not derive its values from the world.

Devotion is dedication. Dedication gives a devotee his self-fulfilment. Self-fulfilment is God's infinitude.

Unlike others, a devotee sincerely feels that he

has nothing else in his Possession save his desire for God. His desire is his jewel. God's Grace is His jewel. In offering his jewel to God, the devotee binds God. In giving His jewel to His devotee, God liberates and fulfils him.

8. Surrender

Surrender knows that there is a guiding Hand and feels that this guiding Hand is ever present. This Hand may strike or bless the aspirant. The surrendered aspirant has discovered the truth that whatever comes from the Supreme is always fruitful of Good and Light.

In life, everything may fail us, but not surrender. Surrender has a free access to God's omnipotence. Hence the path of surrender is the perfect perfection of protection.

Surrender has the strength to meet the Absolute and stay and play with Him eternally. God may at times play hide-and-seek with man's other divine qualities, but never with His devotee's genuine surrender.

Inner surrender transforms life into an infinite progress. It gives life the soulful assurance that life lives in God and God alone.

Surrender is the soul of the devotee's body. Surrender is the unparallelled fulfilment of the devotee's life. Surrender takes him to the Source. When he is in the Source, he becomes the Highest and reveals the Deepest.

Individuality hates surrender. Surrender illumines individuality. Individuality is self-will. Self-will is self-love. Surrender is God-Will. God-Will is God-Love.

Surrender is the purest devotion that sees through the eye of intuition. Surrender is freedom, perpetual freedom, for it always stays with God, in God and for God.

The eye of surrender does not see the face of the Hostile Forces. It always sees the Face of God's Compassion, Protection and Divinity. The life of surrender divinely rings true. It is always filled with abiding inspiration, revealing aspiration and transcending realisation.

Surrender is the wisdom that sees and becomes the Truth. Surrender wishes nothing other than God. Surrender gets pure God. Nothing is as practical as surrender, for it knows the supreme secret that to offer itself integrally to God is to possess God absolutely.

> Surrender clings to God with all the might of the soul.
> Surrender clings to God with all the love of

the heart.
Surrender clings to God with all the will of the mind.
Surrender clings to God with all the dynamic energy of the vital.
Surrender clings to God with all the snow-white emotions of the body.

9. Occultism and spirituality, part 1

The occult power is taught, as it were, in God's private Primary School; the spiritual power in His High School; the omnipotent Will in His University.

An occultist, in wielding his power from one plane to another, flies faster than sound. The Yogi, embracing each plane of consciousness, marches forward more confidently than a commander.

The occultist, fighting endless battles for supremacy over the vital planes of consciousness, develops a rigid and inflexible mind. Difficult, if not impossible, is it for him to have an amenable and adaptable consciousness. The Yogi alone knows how to attain an inner level of poise. He alone can embrace the Infinite.

An occult power and a spiritual freedom often fight shy of each other. Occult power is a restricted force used to serve a particular purpose. Spiritual freedom reveals the universal consciousness in its vast totality.

The march of time bows to the occultist; the glory of distance surrenders to him; the secrets of humanity prostrate before him. Yet strangely enough, the occultist himself finds no escape. He, too, has to sit at the feet of the Omniscient Vision and the Omnipotent Will.

10. Occultism and spirituality, part 2

The Occultist says, "God is a deer."
The Yogi says, "God is also a tortoise."
The Occultist says, "God is Power."
The Yogi says, "God is also Peace."
The Occultist says, "In my victory, God Himself applauds."
The Yogi says, "In my victory, God's Face is a sweet smile."
The Occultist says, "To me, fear has no existence."
The Yogi says, "To me, even impossibility has no existence."
The Occultist says, "My strength is God's dynamic Will."
The Yogi says, "My strength is God's all-sustaining Poise."
The Occultist says, "My speciality lies in my one-pointed Will."
The Yogi says, "My speciality lies in my transformed consciousness."

He is truly a divine warrior who uses not only his occult power as a sword, but also his spiritual power as a shield.

The occult powers used by most primitive tribes are those capacities lying latent in man's unlit vital nature. They are used to propitiate and battle the beings and elements of the vital worlds. As human evolution is now proceeding along mental lines, most men are no longer interested in the vital plane and have lost the capacity to function there. Generally, they are no longer fascinated by the spell of the vital worlds. Humanity now cares little for the powers below the mind, aspiring, as it does, for a truth and light far above it.

Oh, Black Magician, to me, you are a snake-charmer! If you know the art, the snake becomes your toy. If you err, its venom will reduce you to a piteous victim.

What exactly is "black magic"? It is a violent art which has nothing to do with the Divine Will. It can never elevate man's consciousness, even by a fraction. On the contrary, it ruthlessly harms and blights the consciousness, first of the victim, and later of the magician himself.

Just as it is impossible for a man to square the

circle, so is it impossible for an occultist to live always in the sea of divine Peace.

Look at the eyes of an Occultist. He is likely to look care-laden. Look at the eyes of a Yogi. You are likely to observe that peace and serenity flood his atmosphere. Where indeed is the choice between the Occultist's intensity and the Yogi's immensity?

11. Philosophy

All riddles of life can be unriddled, for a sweet concord in secret sports within us mortals.

It is a true truth that life was fast asleep in matter, and mind was fast asleep in life; now without the least hesitation we can say that something lies fast asleep in mind. The wheel of evolution ever moves – it stops not.

Fast asleep in mind lies the Consciousness Divine, fully illumined and patiently awaiting the moment of its unveiling.

When will Nature stop working? She will stop working only when she sees Immortality marching across the giant breast of Death.

Matter is the pride of Europe. Spirit is the pride of India. Neither of the two can possess a complete satisfaction, for the former is in the dark about the potentialities of the Spirit, and the latter about the cogency of Matter. There can be no abiding happiness until Matter and Spirit are amalgamated into one Reality.

Agnosticism is of various types. Fruitful agnosticism has every right to its own teeming knowledge. It is from agnosticism that we come to suspect that an Unknowable Reality engenders all our values: physical, intellectual and spiritual.

We ought to feel extremely happy at the thought that materialism today is no longer an impediment to our upward journey. At most it has the power to make us suffer an indefinite delay. True knowledge has become its soul's real need.

If we cast aside the pall of ignorance and don the robe of knowledge, we find matter, life and mind to be nothing but energy. Though each has a world of its own, there is no yawning chasm separating them.

From its very beginning, Consciousness has been consumed with the snow-white desire to bestow on man a deathless Life, an infinite Knowledge, and an omnipotent Power.

God, the Inner Pilot, hides within us with His Vision of Unity, Omniscience and Omnipotence. And in His own time, He will appear before us. Doubtless we are ignorant of our ultimate aim. Yet for all our ignorance, we are proceeding in all our activities towards our Goal.

12. Realisation

Experience is a rented house, while Realisation is a permanent Palace.

If you have sincerity, God-realisation becomes easy. And in addition to sincerity, if you have patience, God-realisation becomes easier. And in addition to sincerity and patience, if you have self-sacrifice, God-realisation becomes the easiest.

A perfect renunciation and a complete self-surrender are the obverse and reverse of an ambrosial coin.

As the prayer, so the answer. As the sacrifice, so the reward. As the realisation, so the union.

What does liberation teach you? It teaches you that like *Purusha, Prakriti* is also above all disturbances, although she is to be found ever in the whirlwind of work.

An individual perfection and liberation are far from God's supreme and ultimate intention. What He wants is the universalisation of the individual perfection and liberation.

13. Immortality

Consciousness is the only truth that is immortal in mortality.

Speech is the bosom friend of fleeting moments; Silence, the Lover of Eternity.

Hell welcomes the ill-doer. Heaven welcomes the man of virtue. The fulfilment of Immortality welcomes the realised man.

The gods are the divinely individualised branches of the all-sheltering and all-protecting Tree, the Supreme.

An ordinary life plays with ignorance. A religious life plays with rites and ceremonies. A spiritual life plays with the inner planes of consciousness. A divinely transformed life will play with the consciousness of Immortality.

Self-realisation is only the childhood of the greatest Yogi's Immortality.

What is Immortality? Immortality does not mean that we shall be granted an indefinite prolongation of life with all our human desires fulfilled for the asking. The true Immortality is to live in the Divine and to possess the Divine Consciousness.

14. The Guru, part 1

The man-Guru shows you the Throne of the Infinite. The God-Guru makes you sit on the Throne.

The Guru is at once the sigh of unaspiring disciples and the ecstasy of aspiring disciples.

A real Guru is the selfless, dedicated and eternal beggar who begs omnipotence and omnipresence from God to feed his unconsciously hungry and consciously aspiring disciples, in perfect conformity with their souls' needs.

The Guru has only one compassionate Weapon: Forgiveness. The disciple has three naked swords: Limitation, Weakness and Ignorance. Nevertheless, the Guru wins with great ease.

A man may have hundreds of companions. But a spiritual seeker has only one companion: his Preceptor.

The Guru is the one who closes the Door at the Will of God and opens It to the tears of the disciple.

When you go to a doctor, you must tell him all

about the disease you have been suffering from. Otherwise he will not be able to help you fully. Likewise you must make a clean breast of your errors and misdeeds to your Guru. Mere acceptance of a Guru, while you secretly move and act at your sweet will, can be of no avail.

There is no better way for a disciple to serve his Guru than to listen to his advice.

He alone is the real disciple who finds no wrong in his Guru. Being one with the Guru, he discovers his Guru's Consciousness to be perpetual molasses and he himself a lump of transformed sugar.

The Guru is at once the source of his disciple's achievements and a most faithful servant of his disciple's love.

The Guru and the disciple must test each other sweetly, seriously and perfectly before their mutual acceptance. Otherwise, if they are wrong in their selection, the Guru will have to dance with failure and the disciple with perdition.

The Guru is the consolation for the disciple's despair; also is he the compensation for the disciple's loss, if there be any, during the seeker's endless journey towards the all-fulfilling Goal.

The Guru's love for his disciple is his strength. The disciples' surrender towards his Guru is his strength.

The Mother aspect of the Guru is sacrifice.

The Father aspect of the Guru is compassion.

The Guru is not the body. The Guru is the revelation and manifestation of a Divine Power upon earth.

15. The Guru, part 2

All berries are not edible. Likewise all are not Gurus that men may flock to.

What does the acceptance of a disciple by a Guru mean? It means that the Guru will gladly live in the world of golden sacrifice.

If the disciple discovers within himself the pangs of fear and not the fount of love for his Guru, sorrow and spiritual frustration will dog him throughout his discipleship.

The Guru sees in his disciple the very image of God. So he is all sacrifice to the disciple. The disciple sees and feels in his Guru the only shelter of his limitations. So he is all love for his Guru.

The Guru can kindle the lamp in you. When? Only after you have brought him the wick and the oil.

O disciple! Do you know the most foolish customer on earth? He is your Guru and your Guru alone. He buys your ignorance and gives you knowledge; he buys your impotence and gives you power. Can you ever imagine a more foolish bargain? Now learn the name of your

Guru's foolishness: Compassion and nothing else.

The Guru's body is the Compassion-Net. It entraps the disciples, sleeping or awakened, with all their baffling age-long problems of ignorance.

It has become a fashion nowadays for man to say that there is no necessity of an intermediary between him and God, referring not only to the traditional priest, but also to the traditional Guru. Granted, but just tell me: did you receive any help in learning the alphabet? Did you require a teacher to help you master your musical instrument? Were you given instruction to enable you to obtain your degree? If you needed a helper to do these things, do you not also require a teacher who can guide you to the knowledge of the Divine, the wisdom of the Infinite? That teacher is your Guru and no one else.

O man, do you have no love for the temple inside which you worship the idol? Then you must love the body of the Guru, if you aspire to worship the Omnipotent in him.

To achieve realisation oneself and alone is like crossing the ocean in a raft. But to achieve realisation through the Grace of a Guru is like crossing the Ocean in a swift and strong boat, which ferries you safely across the sea of ignorance to the Golden Shore.

Who can show a disciple his true Motherland? The Guru. What is the name of that Motherland? Consciousness: Consciousness Infinite, Consciousness All-Pervading.

The real work, if there be any, of a Guru is to show the world that his deeds are in perfect harmony with his teachings.

16. The soul

Each soul is not only an important page in the Book of Fate, but also essential to it, for without it the Book must needs be incomplete.

Each soul is a representative and a presentation of the Supreme on earth. When the representative is recognised by its owner, the presentation fulfils itself in the Supreme.

The soul comes into birth for experience. And its experience will be complete when it brings down all the perfection of the Divine into Matter.

God touches Matter. Lo, the miracle of miracles: the psychic being comes into existence. Earth-consciousness is the Mother of the child, which develops into an individuality perfected and guided by the Supreme Himself.

The psychic being stores up the quintessence of past experiences and it has very little to do with form and personality.

The Promised Land is for him who perpetually lives in the widening pastures of the soul.

Selfless emotion has an appreciable function of its own. When it knocks, the psychic being cannot help opening the door.

Whenever our soul gets the opportunity of breaking open the door of our ignorance, it speaks in silence to our wakeful mind: "Think not of today's failure, but concentrate on tomorrow's victory."

The smile of our soul is the inner strength given to our life to brave the buffets of unavoidable adversity.

The vital can sit at most at the foot of the mountain; the mind near the top of the mountain; the soul sits right on the peak.

In the relationship between the human soul and the Divine soul, the former embraces, the Latter blesses.

Our sleeping mind feels God as an inexpressible sigh. Our soul feels God as an unexpressed All-Loving Smile.

17. Transformation

Neither an individual effort nor an individual abnegation can bring about the transformation of your consciousness. This transformation is possible only by the descent of a Higher Light.

To think of physical transformation without having some kind of realisation is to count your chickens before they are hatched.

Surrender has to look up with folded hands. Transformation has to look down with palms facing the earth-consciousness.

The transformation of human nature in its completeness must unavoidably progress at the speed of a tortoise.

Both the descent of Truth into the lower nature and the ascent of the lower nature into the higher Truth are capable of solving the problem of problems, the illumination of human consciousness. They are equally effective and have an equal speed.

Be universal in your love. You will see the universe to be the picture of your own being.

There is but one Knowledge. There is but one Realisation. You are at once the Seeker and the

Fulfiller.

What is liberation? It is the extinction of a divided consciousness in the all-pervading oneness of the Supreme.

What is meant by spiritual perfection? It is the constant capacity to live in God and to reveal Him in one's every moment.

In the field of true spirituality, Experience serves as breakfast; Realisation as lunch; Transformation as dinner.

18. The consciousness of history

From time immemorial, History has been dealing with tyrants and liberators. Before long, it will have to deal seriously with peacemakers.

History is the fountain-head of man's moments of self-expression, drawn from his conscious or unconscious choice of forces in the world.

When man chooses the force of Truth, ever at play on earth's atmosphere, he aligns himself with evolution's greatest power.

When he allows himself to become the instrument of the force of Darkness, he becomes the ally of evolution's greatest regressive agent.

Both the beauty of truth and the ugliness of falsehood have an ever-failing friend: History.

History ever drifts from the wind of an imponderable sigh to the sunshine of a stupendous smile.

Who has eyes that look backward even when they consciously look forward? The deep-penetrating dweller in the core of History.

What is History, after all? Is it not merely what man has chosen to regard as important? History has been until now a record of man's values. But the time will soon come when it will become a record of God's values, a study of man's growth from blind infancy to the full maturity of enlightened spirituality.

19. Concentration and meditation

Concentration is the Arrow.
Meditation is the Bow.

When you concentrate, you focus all your energies upon the chosen phenomenon in order to unveil its mysteries. When you meditate, you rise into a higher consciousness.

Concentration wants to penetrate into the object it strives for. Meditation wants to live in the vastness of Silence.

In concentration, you endeavour to bring the consciousness of your object right into your own awareness. In meditation, you rise from your limited consciousness into a higher and wider domain.

If you want to sharpen your faculties, concentrate. If you want to lose yourself, meditate.

It is the work of concentration to clear the roads when meditation wants to go either deep within or high above.

Concentration wants to seize the knowledge it aims at. Meditation wants to identify itself with the knowledge it seeks for.

An aspirant has two genuine teachers: Concentration and Meditation. Concentration is always strict with the student; Meditation is strict at times. But both of them are solemnly interested in their students' progress.

Concentration says to God: "Father, I am coming to You." Meditation says to God: "Father, do come to me."

Concentration is the commander who orders the dispersed consciousness to come to attention.

Concentration and absolute firmness are not only inseparable, but are interdependent divine warriors.

Concentration does not allow Disturbance, the thief, to enter into his armoury. Meditation lets him in. Why? Just to catch the thief red-handed.

Concentration challenges the enemy to a duel and fights him out. Meditation, with its silent smile, diminishes the challenge of the enemy.

Concentration and the surface mind dislike each other. Concentration opens the door to higher states of consciousness, while the surface mind wants to stay where it has always been.

The mind that is incapable of concentration is as changeable as the wind and as elusive as moonlight.

When concentration reaches its acme, revelation dawns. Newton saw the law of gravitation in the falling of an apple; Archimedes discovered the secret of displacement and cried out, "Eureka!"; JC Bose discovered life in plants, even in metals. The crown of success is attainable only in moments of deepest concentration.

20. Prosperity and adversity

Prosperity and Adversity are the two eyes that we all have. Adversity leads us inward to correct and perfect our march of life. Prosperity leads us outward to illuminate and immortalise our human birth.

In prosperity our inner strength remains static. In adversity our inner strength becomes dynamic.

None can deny the fact that every step of progress which the world has made has come from both the smiles of prosperity and the tears of adversity.

Adversity, like poverty, is no sin. One merit of adversity none can deny: it helps us to be stronger within. The stronger we are within, the brighter we are without.

"No suffering, no salvation," so says the teacher Adversity to his student, man.

"No soul's delight, no salvation," so says the teacher Prosperity to his student, man.

One who is afraid of studying in the school of adversity can never hope for a perfect education in life.

Misfortune threatens prosperity.
Hope ignores adversity.

How often is our aspiration forced into play by dire adversity; but in glorious prosperity how rarely it peeps out.

No fall, no rise. Just as a wrestler often bears away the prize only after he has suffered numerous falls, even so Hell is to be experienced before Heaven is won.

What is failure, if not an important portion, unrecognised, in the configuration of our whole fruitful success?

Failure can have a soothing medicine to relieve it from its pangs, and that medicine is consolation. Failure can have an energising medicine to relieve it from its pangs, and that medicine is Will-power.

The world is strewn with difficulties. In a sense, it is full of thorns. But if you put on shoes you can walk on the thorns. What are these shoes made of? They are made of God's Grace.

Depression is the most effective smile of a wrong force. Once we allow it to enter, depression tries to crush the strength and joy of our life-force.

Illness often has very little to do with the Divine Will. It is rather the acceptance of imperfection's invasion.

The pain of the body is often bearable. Not so is the pain of the heart.

Sorrow is an arrow to pierce into strength. Joy is food to feed strength sumptuously.

Sorrow lords it over the world. But the very presence of Time makes it lose its sting.

Time is the best physician for suffering. Then comes patience. And then comes tolerance.

Man is the visible hyphen between yesterday's torture and tomorrow's fear.

Natural justice, however painful, is mild. Legal justice, however mild, is atrocious torture.

Despair is an unworthy and shameless guest of our inner life. We must resist it with the current of will that energises our soul.

Disappointment is as powerful a negative force as expectation is a positive one.

Worry unconsciously welcomes trouble. Trouble unavoidably welcomes helplessness.

Helplessness tearfully welcomes despair.

    Human life is at once a burden and a blessing. It compels man to bear continual suffering. It gives man also a great promise of God-Realisation.

21. Matter and spirit

True wisdom must dawn on human consciousness. Affirmations and negations must be synthesised and move together. The world has come to realise that integrality is the only absolute self-fulfilment.

Neither Spirit nor Matter is superior to the other. We will be far from Truth if we belittle Matter only to speak highly of Spirit. From Matter alone did our earthly cloak see the light of day.

To the materialist, the Beyond is unreal because it is not within his eye-range. He has enquired of his senses if they were aware of the Beyond. They unanimously cried out: "No, there is no such thing!"

The Spirit, untouched and uncontaminated by imperfection, is the sole gateman of the Transcendent. Radiant and immaculate, it bears and upholds the world. Relation it has none. Its matchless qualities are the opposites of division, duality and multiplicity.

The eternal Truth can never be the monopoly of the Spirit. Dauntless Matter, too, has every right to claim her equal share.

Our present faith in Matter is not enough. It must needs be stronger. We must see eye to eye with the Upanishads and declare that Matter also is Brahman.

Our absolute Freedom will come into existence from the Spirit. But Matter's giant breast will be the field of our full manifestation.

The materialist is aware of the road that leads to matter. He is quite in the dark about the road that leads to the spirit. It seems that the Eternal Solace is extremely clever. It deserts both the materialist and the spiritualist en route when they want to be independent of each other.

Materialism has begun to far exceed the limits of sense-knowledge. With this obstruction fading away, the march of materialism is now quite safe and satisfactory towards its unimagined Goal.

The supreme choice of an awakened mind is an unalloyed affirmation of the soul's light pouring into the mental vehicle.

Multiplicity is nothing but the outer robe of unity.

What is the most essential thing in our upward and inward march? Faith. Faith is the bud; knowledge is the flower. O Faith! Since you are the ceaseless breath of our hearts, we feel that before long we must win the crown of our journey's Goal.

What is Silence? Silence is that which alone bears the teeming vast. It upholds activity and inactivity in its own supreme delight and places the garlands of victory around the necks of these two apparent antagonists.

"All this is Brahman." The oneness of Matter and Spirit is the only affirmation of the Brahman. Therefore neither Matter nor Spirit can dwell beyond its fond and boundless clasp.

22. Spiritual discipline

Any method of spiritual discipline will have two inevitable and inseparable wings: absolute patience and firm resolution.

A progressive self-giving and an absolute confidence in God can easily challenge the strength of impossibility in one's spiritual journey.

March forward just three steps and God is won. Now what are the three steps? The first step is aspiration. The second step is self-giving. The third step is reliance on oneself, reliance on the Divine.

In the early stages of spiritual practice, to leave everything to the Divine and to think that personal effort is unnecessary is to dance before you can walk.

Tapasya [intense or austere discipline] says to the aspirant: "I shall make you see God." Surrender says to the aspirant: "I shall make God see you."

Faithfulness is the only key that both Tapasya and Surrender possess to open God's door.

In the ultimate analysis, no distinction can

ever be made between Tapasya and Surrender. Surrender, when complete and effective, is the result of, and nothing other than the most arduous Tapasya.

The more complete the aspirant's surrender, the brighter the smile of his psychic being.

Surrender is fondly influenced by the psychic being. Knowledge is boldly influenced by the Will.

Surrender is the most suitable net to entrap the Divine. It is at once wisdom and power in action.

Spontaneous obedience is the husk. Conscious surrender is the rice.

Demanding surrender says to God: "Father, I am looking at You. Be pleased to look at me. Let us look at each other." Devoted surrender says to God: "Father, I need not look at You. You just look at me. That will do."

There are three ways of fulfilling a soul's need: either the aspirant steps forward to see the Divine; or the Divine steps forward to make the aspirant see Him; or both the aspirant and the Divine step forward simultaneously towards each other.

When the aspirant bitterly starves his questioning mind and feeds his surrender sumptuously, God says: "The time is ripe. I come."

Surrender can never be a one-day achievement. Likewise realisation, when attained, is not a one-day wonder.

Although regularity in spiritual practice may appear mechanical, it is a constant blessing from above and shows the development of some inner strength.

To see God only during your surrender at meditation is to declare that God is absent from you more than He is present.

True meditation has a free access to the inner Being. True self-consecration has a free access to the right consciousness and attitude.

When the mind and the vital close their eyes for good, surrender, the inner strength, opens its eyes for good.

23. Humility

The seed of humility is exceptionally fertile. It may not germinate plants of power and force, but it does yield flowers of Sweetness, Grace, Modesty and Light.

Love for the Divine is in its essence a spontaneous spiritual humility.

Humility has no need to sit on the King's throne. But the King cannot help bringing the throne to humility. And now who is the King? God's Compassion.

A prayer, in its simplest and most effective definition, is humility, climbing the sky of an all-fulfilling Delight.

Only the true sense of humility can raise us from our knees as high as we aspire.

We must realise that there is only one way of acquiring infinite future possibilities. That way lies in the great power: Humility.

24. Admiration

Admiration is not the sign of inferiority. Rather it is often a sign of the reciprocal recognition of two souls.

Familiarity and admiration can rarely be long-enduring friends, unless the uniqueness of the one finds an echo in the other.

It is easy for our admiration to win over another's love. But often it is too difficult for our love to win over another's admiration.

Can one separate our admiration from our sincerity? Decidedly not. For admiration demands a truthful selflessness.

Self-love must know that its annihilation will begin when admiration enters.

Admiration begins to show the psychic touch when it reaches out towards those eternal qualities possessed by seers, saints and sages.

25. Ambition

Ambition is the fond embrace of possession and expression.

Life is an ever-progressing reality. This is the firm conviction of ambition.

If your ambition is to achieve perfection, then do not destroy imperfection. The destruction of imperfection can never be the way to perfection.

Ambition is an attempt at self-expression and self-extension. When it is based on the ego's enlargement, we call it self-aggrandisement. When it is based on the soul's illumination, it ceases to be ambition and becomes a divine Mission.

26. Character

Among the fearless soldiers that fight for your victory in life, character has no equal.

Character is the colossal hope of human improvement within and without.

Character is blazing sunshine in the soul's abode, the body.

A perfect society is built upon mutual trust. Character is the source of that trust.

Character is just what we inwardly are and outwardly do.

The secret of inner success is constancy to our highest character.

A true aspirant is one who feels more and more cautious of the least ignorance and limitation in himself.

Character gives the key to open the most beautiful doors of life: Peace of Mind and Delight.

Self-discipline is the foundation of a moral human life on earth. Self-sacrifice will be the foundation of a supra-moral life on earth.

27. Courage

Courage is the most devoted servant of one's own faith in oneself and God.

Timidity says, "God is forever unknowable." Courage says, "God is at present unknown, but only for a while."

Cowardice is an extra load to carry in the march of your day-to-day life.

Courage is an ever-willing extra porter to carry your wealth, inner and outer, according to your soul's volition.

Courage is perfection only when it springs from one's oneness with the vision of God.

There is no other way to please your inner self than to be, yourself, a perfect emblem of courage.

Enthusiasm in its purest expression is courage.

Without courage, life is a path without progress.

Against one's inner courage, death itself contends in vain.

Courage is God's successful inspiration in Man's body, mind, heart and soul.

28. Equanimity

Equanimity is the hyphen between God's Compassion and man's surrender.

Equanimity is the all-covering, all-protecting umbrella of true wisdom.

Whatever takes place in the divine Providence is not only for the best, but also inevitable, because there is no alternative.

A realised soul is he who is above likes and dislikes. He lives in the world cheerfully, but he is not of it.

Equanimity can by no means imply an inert acceptance. Far from it, equanimity is the living faith of a seeker in the divine Dispensation.

To be able to endure the buffets of life firmly and calmly is to have the full taste of matchless equanimity.

To take the inevitable, unmoved, for our Goal is a divine blessing.

29. Purity and power

Have purity first; then only will you never be devoid of power.

Look at the miracle of a drop of venom and a drop of purity. The former poisons the blood in your veins. The latter purifies the human soul in your body.

Power is not necessarily purity, but purity is sheer power.

There is no one who can fly as high as a divine dispenser of power. There is no man who can ruin his heart as quickly as a misuser of power.

To have experiences without the strength of purification is like living in the most dangerous part of the forest. This does not mean that experience must always wait for complete purification. What is actually needed is a good understanding and a true relation between growing experience and growing purification.

Knowledge is a secret power. When you have won knowledge, power is bound to follow it.

Purity is the ceaseless shower of God's omnipotent Grace on aspiring human souls.

Purity is the immediate gift from the universal Treasure-House to God's hopeful children.

30. India: Her Consciousness and Light, part 1

What is India's spiritual message to the world at large? Spirituality. What is spirituality? It is the natural way of truth that successfully communes with the Beyond here on earth.

What is India's absolutely distinctive possession? Her soul. She lives in the soul, she lives from the soul and lives for the soul.

Where can the world find the real nature of India? In the ever-wakeful domain of the Spirit.

What has made the history of India unique? The most surprisingly unusual continuity of the line of her spiritual seekers and Masters.

What does Indian spirituality teach? It teaches the world to conquer the evil of the lower nature and also to go beyond the good of the higher nature.

Has Mother India any desire? If so, what is it? It is to transcend the human way once and for all, in the ever dynamic way of God, in the way of radical self-transmutation.

Religion, however mighty it may be, is not

and cannot be the message of India. Her message is self-realisation.

The perfect truth of India's religion is in her outer and inner realisation of the One that is, of the One that is in the process of becoming.

O world, on you march towards the deepest recesses of your heart! To your amazement, you will find Mother India to be anything but God-fearing. What then is she? She is God-loving! The God-loving soul in God's all-dreaming and all-manifesting Truth.

The soul of India feels that to be satisfied with intellectual speculation is to remain satisfied with half of the food that is actually needed for health. It is Realisation that gives one a full meal. And to have the Realisation, meditation and concentration are of paramount importance.

Indian philosophy, in its sublimest sense, is nothing short of the practical realisation of the Truth.

There is just a hyphen between the Vision of the Vedic seers and the soul of India. Also between India's spirituality and the final spiritual liberation of the world.

31. India: Her Consciousness and Light, part 2

They say that India long ago lost the Milky Way of greatness. But we know that she has now a colossal hope that the overcast sky will clear at last, revealing again the myriad points of light.

What were the chief causes of India's downfall? She neglected the body-consciousness and eschewed the material life; she narrowed her outlook and sealed herself up in the outworn rituals of the past; she clung to the festering shell of her ancient culture and succeeded in killing its living, growing spirit. And India's doom was sealed the day she started these practices.

India began to rise the day she turned away from these tendencies and accepted life in all its dynamic aspects.

India will rise fully the day she becomes self-reliant. She knows well that she cannot achieve her goal if she has to depend permanently on alien help. Self-help is the best help. Self-help is God's own help in disguise.

India has within her a voice that is the self-same, all-fulfilling voice of God. That voice she simply must hear and act up to.

What is actually meant by the emancipation of the Indian woman? It means that she must no longer be alienated from education. She must have free access to the world-wide knowledge of the present day, in addition to the sacred lore of the past centuries. True education helps us to live in the integral perfection which is the very backbone of our existence on earth. The Indian woman must be given a full opportunity to develop and manifest this perfection.

True, consumed with desires and temptations, Europe rushed towards India to acquire her fabulous wealth. It is equally and absolutely true that Europe's soul came to India with a spiritual seeking and an occult urge to discover what India was actually like.

India has three world-conquering weapons: Non-Violence, Peace and the Wisdom that tells that she is in All as All is in her.

India's choice is character. But she must feel that she needs personality as well.

Mother India's fear is not in atomic bombs but in her children's Self-forgetful amnesia.

Unbelievably, India has perfectly reconciled in herself the two worst antagonists: Renunciation and Epicurianism.

Perfection was the choice of the Greeks. Proportion was the choice of the Romans. Universality is the choice of the Indians.

India is the voice that never falters. Hers is the truth that cannot be silenced by the threatening darkness of centuries. Hers is the heart that sings perpetually the unity of mankind.

India is the vault of an ancient eternal wisdom that has a universal appeal. She is also the universal reserve-bank of an ever-growing wisdom and is destined to be the hub and dynamo of world transformation.

32. Truth and true Knowledge

A theory must be tested. A fact must be honoured. A truth must be lived.

What is joy today may be sorrow tomorrow. But what is Truth today cannot be Falsehood tomorrow.

There are truths that cannot be expressed in words. Likewise there are truths that should not be expressed untimely in words.

There has been a very long-enduring tug-of-war between two parties. One party consists of Truth, Freedom and Immortality. The other party consists of Falsehood, Bondage and Death. Until now the world has seen God weeping through the eyes of the first party.

Our very life is an ambition to fight out obscurity and ignorance.

The more we inwardly obey, the better we outwardly rule.

Perfection is the conscious annihilation of one's egocentric self.

To a dauntless soul, life is indeed an enjoyable serpentine winding of the road leading to Truth.

Sacrifice and Freedom-in-Will can and should peacefully move together to reach the palace of Truth.

Teach or preach the Ultimate Truth on its own level. If you reduce it to the footing of a particular listener to make it accessible to his understanding, the power and strength of that Truth will be lost.

Ignorance, however abysmal, always has within it some seeds of truth, however twisted and incomplete. Knowledge, however exalted, until it founds itself in the Gnostic Consciousness, always contains some element of ignorance.

Go deep within yourself and to your great surprise, you will find ignorance. It is a kind of knowledge, of course, but infinitely far from all-fulfilling. Go deep within yourself and to your utter astonishment, you will find knowledge. It is a kind of ignorance, of course, but holding within itself the seeds of True Wisdom.

Ignorance says, "You and I, I and you."

Knowledge says, "You within me, I within you."

To be sure, the state of ignorance is a conscious, groping aspect of Knowledge in the Divine.

To be conscious means to be aware of the unrealities that go to make one's nature limited and imperfect.

Unconsciousness, the mentor, allows us to be mere blind instruments. Consciousness, the mentor, teaches us how to be pure, knowing agents.

From the birth of man, ignorance has been trying to throw Wisdom into the shade. But Wisdom never retaliates. On the contrary, Wisdom gives ignorance its due value.

Just as education has not made much headway among certain backward groups, even so the cultivation of Self-Knowledge has not made much headway among ill-lit humanity.

Self-revelation is the victorious smile of spontaneous progress.

The vanity of worldly wisdom cannot be removed by ripe old age. It can be removed only by our self-illumination.

In the intensity of love, we can extend our

Knowledge and follow the footsteps of God.

If you want bliss, then seek Truth for Truth's sake alone.

Truth is your Goal. If necessary, get to it even through Hell.

Truth expressed, beauty and love fulfilled.

Everything has death pre-destined for it, save the all-commanding dignity of Truth.

Every falsehood eventually dies in Truth, but Truth once revealed never dies.

33. Life

Life is love.
Love is life.
Life fulfils God through love.
Love fulfils God in life.

Life has an inner door. Aspiration opens it. Desire closes it. Aspiration opens the door from within. Desire closes it from without.

Life has an inner lamp. This inner lamp is called aspiration. And when we keep our aspiration burning, it will, without fail, transmit to God's entire creation its effulgent glow.

Life has an inner Voice. This Voice is the Light of the Supreme. Life is protection, life is perfection, life is fulfilment when we open to this Light of the Supreme.

Each day is the renewal of life. Each day is the rebirth of our inner assurance that each individual is the chosen instrument of the Supreme to reveal and fulfil the infinite Divine here on earth.

The outgoing life finds nothing but trouble, torture, misery and frustration. The inflowing life discovers the Sea of peace and bliss.

How to start life's inner journey? With the simple idea, the spontaneous thought that God-Realisation is your birthright. Where to start? Here. From within. When to start? Now. Before the birth of a second.

To illumine our life we need pure thoughts. Each pure thought is more precious than all the diamonds of the world, for God's Breath abides only in man's pure thoughts.

Life is always at work. It is ever active, dynamic. It tries to help the soul to complete its yet unaccomplished task, the divine Mission. The soul needs life's help to unfold itself fully. Life needs the soul's help to fulfil itself both physically and spiritually.

Birth and death play. They play together. Their game is the game of harmony. And it is always played on the infinite breast of Life.

Brooding and despondency are the worst foes to kill life in all its divine inspiration. No more brooding, no more despondency. Your life shall become the beauty of a rose, the song of the dawn, the dance of the twilight.

God is in life. But life must awaken to the light of His Presence, His Transcendent Feet.

34. Death

Death is natural. Nothing natural can be detrimental. Death is rest. Rest is strength in disguise for a further adventure.

At the present state of human evolution, to conquer Death may be an impossibility. But to overcome the fear of death is not only practicability, but inevitability.

Death is normally the sign that the soul, under the particular circumstances, has exhausted the possibilities of its progress in a particular body.

When the strength of possibility loses to the strength of impossibility, it is called Death.

A useless life is a cordial invitation to Death.

Death is the hyphen between man's growing fear and his shrinking life-energies.

He who prefers Death to Life has only to climb up the Tree. But he who prefers Life to Death has not only to climb up, but also to climb down again to do God's work.

When Death approaches a man, his psychic being says to Death, "Death, just wait, let me see what I wish to work out in the next birth."

Death says, "You want life, evolutionary growth. Sorry, you are asking a favour from the wrong person. One second's delay on my part may add something to your experience!"

Death says that it is immortal. Man's achievements say, "Death, you are right. But the truth of the matter is that we shine perpetually upon your very breast. Not only that, we shine forever in you, through you and beyond you."

35. The seeker

What am I? I am a climbing cry. Who am I? God's ever-expanding sky.

If you seek God in God's own Ways, you will meet God as fulfilment. If you seek God in other ways, you will meet God as frustration.

An ordinary man must think logically and act sensibly to prove himself worth living. A spiritual seeker must think intuitively and act divinely to prove himself worth living.

A bridge of steel spans a mighty river. And what is needed to build that bridge? A combination of a creative brain and a vast mathematical knowledge. A bridge of sacrifice spans Heaven and Earth. And what is needed to build that bridge? A combination of God's Compassion and the seeker's aspiration.

A sincere seeker of Truth has three inseparable friends: Peace, Faith and Receptivity. Peace says to him: "I shall show you that there is nothing but God." Faith says: "I shall make you see God within you." Receptivity says: "What else is God if not all your life?"

A spiritual seeker must know that austerity is

an abnormality in as much as it is a disturbance of the natural balance of forces in the different parts of our consciousness. Austerity does not give self-mastery. In true detachment is the real self-mastery. Just as Earth has temptations for an ordinary man, so Heaven has temptations for an advanced seeker.

Experience is the open and conscious eye of a seeker. Realisation is the all-seeing eye of a Yogi. To have an experience of truth is to discover at long last an oasis in the desert of life.

"France has more need of me than I of France," said Napoleon. Likewise the world has more need of a realised soul than he of the world.

36. Man

Creation is proud of Man, its crown and peak. Man is proud of his eminence and fulfilment. But in God's vision, even a self-realised man is only the child of the superman to come upon earth.

Man is the son of an ape! But he will be the father of a superman! But how? Both his fast-mounting yearning and the evolving wheel of Life will be responsible for this mighty transformation.

Man is synonymous with impotence. His goal is a far cry from his natural experience. His present is dead in ignorance. But his future will be dead to ignorance. Today brutality gambols within him; tomorrow Divinity.

Alas, man is not aware of the fact that his sweetness and humility go far, yet cost practically nothing.

Man, in essence, is not ugly. But hard is it for a man to appear beautiful, for he has lost the contact with his soul, the child of All-Beauty.

What is it, after all, that gives to a child his charm and beauty? Is it not the soul's glow?

When that touch gets fainter and is finally lost, he becomes a dull and cautious adult.

Man is by nature a lover. Only he has yet to discover the real thing to love. This quest awakens him to the fulfilment of his real Self.

Who is man after all? The one whose eye will make him Eternal, the one whose heart will throb with Immortality.

The man who is a sincere seeker of the Infinite must needs always say: "So little done, so much to do."

Man has two weapons: hope and despair. With hope he tries to kill the stagnation of incapacity. With despair he can kill the birth of the golden future.

If man's life is given for living, then Truth can have its inevitable reason for existing.

Man's joy in forgiving is a joy worth having. Man's joy in being forgiven is a joy worth aspiring for.

Neither admiration nor critical penetration can make one see the secrets of another's life. Self-sacrifice alone can do it.

Man's unseen strength lies in his hopes. His

hope's strength lies in his sacrifice. His sacrifice's strength lies in God's Grace. His Grace's strength is the All-Fulfilling Delight.

37. Man and woman

Equality is a shaky bridge between man and woman. Both man and woman desperately need love and love alone. It is love that is Bliss and never the sense of equality.

Man will be a beggar if he does not get sweetness and sacrifice from woman. Woman will suffer the same fate if she does not get strength and security from man.

If woman's strength is in the beauty of her tears, then man's strength is in the sacrifice of his heart.

If woman's strength is in her silence and reserve, then man's strength is in his vision and action.

If woman's strength is in her quick rejection, then man's strength is in his life's new orientation.

Man thinks of what to say. Woman thinks of how to act.

Man and woman in ignorant love see only one subtle thief: Time. Man and woman in wise love feel only one faithful and inspiring servant: Time.

Man and woman are at their best when they give to each other not only what they have but what they are.

Man brings the message of Heaven. Woman brings the message of Divine Earth. Woman, even in her highest aspect, creates her fulfilment on earth, as *Prakriti*. It is for her to bring the glorious perfection of Heaven to the material base of earth.

Be it in art or literature,
Be it in scholarship or teaching,
Be it in administration and commerce,
Be it in service to society,
Be it in wifehood and motherhood,
Be it in philosophical quest or religious aspiration,
Be it even in spiritual realisation –

Woman is intended by the Supreme to bring the Divine Perfection to earth. Every sphere and aspect of earth, its grossest needs as well as its subtlest nuances, must feel the touch of woman's radiant emanation.

38. Problems and difficulties

We agonise ourselves in trying to make a problem vanish. God laughs at us. But as soon as we accept a difficulty as inevitable, ordained by Him, it slowly melts away until the day comes when we wonder where it has disappeared.

As soon as you have conquered a difficulty, you will find that it repeats itself on a higher and subtler level. It is the same essential weakness in yourself which you are made to face in a more refined form.

A problem exists only in our own consciousness. The same external situation becomes a problem for me but not for you. Why? Because it disturbs some element of my inner harmony, while yours is left untouched.

There is no other way to spiritual success than to sit at the feet of Patience, trusting to her lords, Time and Progress.

Adversity makes you dynamic. Adversity forces your eyes wide open. Adversity teaches you the meaning of patience. Adversity endows you with faith in yourself. Adversity opens the secret door through which you can see the ultimate future fulfilment of God's Will.

Is there any way left for man to be free? Certainly there is. The moment he feels his mind to be a thought of God, he can be at large like a bird in the sky; his life, however fleeting, is a breath of his inner Pilot.

Aspiration can be raised to meet the Peace above; but Peace must be brought down to remove one's difficulties.

Are you casting about for true happiness in life? If so, yield not to reason, yield not to fate, but yield only to the dictates of your Inner Voice.

Difficulty is often fed by its master, Distrust. What is the function of Distrust? Its function is to interfere with the action of the Divine Grace.

An absolute surrender to the Divine is the only strength that can help an aspirant to wrestle with all the outer and inner problems of life.

As our very existence depends on God alone, we must be independent of the values of others, the opinions of others, the demands of others.

Today properly guarded can easily escape tomorrow's snare. It can even nullify yesterday's stumbles.

To think that pain is a well-deserved punishment is wrong. To think that pain is an unavoidable heritage of karma is worse. To think that pain can never be surmounted is worst of all. Pain is a momentary experience of one's limited self before it enters into the sea of Bliss.

39. Art

Creation itself is the Art of arts, although unrecognised.

One truth is clear, very clear. Whatever is, is art. How can any creation of the Supreme Artist be a denial of Him? Even beneath the ugliest and the most loathsome shines His all-loving Face of beauty.

Love is the most charming of all arts. Love is so because it is "life" itself and not the translation of life.

Art is the outer vesture of love. Art, like love, is a force of oneness with the Infinite. When we create a piece of art, we are really re-creating or reflecting some beauty of the Infinite.

Imagination is an essential attribute of the creative power of the mind. It is that son of the mind that sees a thing before it is brought into the material plane.

Imagination, too, has to surrender to its Master: Will. If it is incapable of that, it can never originate anything.

Art is an exacting goddess that demands one's offering of heart, mind and body.

Nature is the mother of an artist. She serves the artist with a presentation of her beauties, visible and invisible.

Nature is the unmistakable evidence of evolutionary growth, and growth is the evidence of life; life, divinely organised and governed, is the evidence of art at its highest.

Keats' address to art: "Thou foster-child of Silence and slow Time" is but half-truth. Art is the child of Silence, no doubt, but it transcends Time.

Beauty without grace is a flower without fragrance.

As man is, after all, an integral being, art has its claim, like knowledge and religion, to be one of his true occupations in life.

Art is creation solidified and concretised.

Art is the joint fulfilment of Truth and Beauty.

Art is the wonderful convincing bridge between the sweetest harmony and the most perfect rhythm.

Physical beauty in a human being is an external manifestation of some inner harmony and truth. This inner beauty is at its highest in the full opening of the soul towards God.

The supreme Art is to know the Supreme Artist intimately, within and without. This knowledge, well-established, cannot but guide all our movements on artistic lines. And this knowledge will be the basis of a perfectly beautiful life within and without. Art in the most effective sense of the term is a sublime truth that draws our soul from within towards the infinite Vast.

40. Aspiration

Aspiration, in its simplest definition, is a lovely flame climbing Heavenward.

True aspiration can and does make us feel that if God is for us, who can eventually stand against us?

We feel a desire to have God on our side. But we need the aspiration to throw ourselves on God's side.

Just as the sun is the only remedy for dark clouds in the sky, similarly, there is no other medicine for our troubled hearts than aspiration.

Aspiration is the first rung of the sky-kissing ladder; Realisation is the last.

True human aspiration has three intimate friends: Purification, Quietude and Intensity. Aspiration has an enemy called impatience.

Aspiration is the mounting flame of our divine wish to raise ourselves to the crest and crowning of Divine Perfection.

The vital aspires through dynamism.
The mind aspires through self-search.

The heart aspires through the feeling of union.
The soul aspires through the perfection of God's manifestation.

41. Grace and compassion

We turn to the Lord for Grace; He looks to us for our sincerity.

A feeble prayer brings down God's omnipotent Grace. Such is the magnanimity of God's Compassion.

To a sincere heart, God's Grace is swifter than a weaver's shuttle. To an insincere heart, it is slower than laziness itself.

God may be unkindness to those who think, but He is All-Kindness to those who feel.

Although man frequently loses faith in God, He never loses His patience. For He knows well that His Grace is destined to save mankind from the tentacles of its own misery.

Our tears to God are our greatest strength to bring down His adamantine protection.

If one wants to be illumined by one word from the lips of God, then that word is Compassion.

Although we are accountable to God for all our conscious and unconscious actions, God, being the Father, finds no better way of dealing with us than to accept, with His benign Compassion, our never-ending errors.

We may not see God personally. But if we can realise the relation between His Grace and His Power, it is as good as seeing Him.

We offer our surrendered helplessness to God from below. He showers blessings on us from above.

God's Grace and God's Justice have been rivals right from the birth of creation. But it goes without saying that His Justice can never keep pace with His Grace.

Aspirant! If evil has an access to the mid-ocean and to the sky, God's all-pervading Compassion has a freer and more embracing access to these places.

Impelled by His strongest Compassion, God takes the feeblest man into His Omnipotence.

The world is partly conscious and partly unconscious of Nature's blessing. Nature is the conscious and direct blessing of God.

Easy is it for a man to say that God has become ruthless towards him. Blessed would be he who would say that God has never been unwise.

In season and out of season we crack venomous jokes. And God simply smiles. But if ever

God cracks a joke – and needless to say, He does so with a set purpose and with the most benevolent intention – we immediately shed bitter tears or become violently angry.

If we think of God's Justice before we think of His Compassion, our hearts will be mistaken. His Justice wants man to be fully exposed, but His Compassion wants to drop a veil over man's follies and misdeeds.

The universe is not vast enough for God's Grace to be buried. Hence It will never disappear.

Our enemy is anger. Anger's enemy is patience. Patience too has an enemy called ignorance. To be sure, eyeless ignorance also has an enemy, although unbelievable. What is it? God's Grace.

The purification of nature by personal effort is to cross over the Sea of Ignorance by a raft. The purification of nature by Grace is to cross over that Sea by an ocean liner.

God's Compassion is that which comes to all, being fully beyond the touch of human wickedness.

God's descending Grace and man's ascending delight are part and parcel of Earth's evolving consciousness.

42. Delight

Delight is the source of existence. Delight is the meaning of existence. Delight is the language of Infinity, Eternity and Immortality.

Delight was our inner past. Delight is our inner present. Delight shall be our inner future. No matter if our outer mind understands not or cares not to understand this self-revealing truth.

Delight is not satisfaction of the mind, the vital and the body. It is something deeper, higher and purer. Delight needs no outer help for its existence. It is self-existent, self-revealing and self-fulfilling.

Delight is the divine bridge between Peace and Power, between Light and Truth, between God's unmanifested Dream and His manifested Reality.

The aggressive, dynamic and apparently conquering vital excitement is not Delight. Delight is surcharged with a creative consciousness which is at once energising, fulfilling and itself fulfilled.

God and I are One when I reach Him through

Delight in the plane of Delight. God is the whole, and I am a portion of Him when I reach Him through my soul's Delight. God is the Boatman and I am the Boat when I reach God through Delight here on earth.

In Delight alone can an aspirant be true to his inmost self. In Delight alone can he feel and understand what God is like. Men speak of God twenty-four hours a day, but not even for a fleeting second do they feel Him, not to speak of understanding Him. If the outer life of an individual can swim in the sea of his soul's Delight, then only will he feel God's Presence, and understand Him in His cosmic Vision and absolute Reality.

High, higher and highest is the plane of Delight. With our illumined consciousness, we rise into that plane and become self-enraptured. Having crossed the corridors of sublime silence and trance, we are now one with the Supreme.

II — Essays, part 1

43. *An experience of Sri Chinmoy at the age of fourteen*

Whenever I had the opportunity, I flew to the edge of the ever-blue sea and took my seat there in solitude. My bird of consciousness, dancing slowly, rose to the sky and lost itself up there.

On that occasion – it was a full-moon night – as I gazed and gazed upon the blue-white horizon, I found only a sea of sweet and serene light. All was engulfed, as it were, in an infinite Ocean of Light which played lovingly on the sweet ripples.

My finite consciousness was in quest of the Infinite and Immortal. I drank deeply of Ambrosia and was floating on an illumined ocean. It seemed that I no longer existed on this earth.

All of a sudden – I do not know why or how – something put an end to my sweet dream. No longer did the air emit its honey-like immortal Bliss, for my own depressed thoughts had come to the fore: "Useless, everything is useless. There is no hope of creating a divine world here on earth. It is only a childish dream." I felt too, that I could not go on even with my own life. This seemed to be nothing but a thorny desert strewn with endless difficulties.

"Why should I suffer these unbearable pains and sorrows here? I am the son of the Infinite. I must have freedom, I must have the ecstasy of Paradise. This ecstasy resides ever within me. Why then should I not leave this mortal world for my Eternal Abode in Heaven?"

A sudden flash of lightning appeared over my head. Looking up with awe and bewilderment, I found above me my Beloved, the King of the Universe, looking at me. His radiant Face was overcast with sorrow.

"Father," I asked, approaching Him, "what makes Thy Face so sad?"

"How can I be happy, My son, if you do not wish to be My companion and help Me in My Mission? I have, concealed in the world, millions of sweet plans which I shall unravel. If My children do not help Me in My play, how can I have

My Divine Manifestation here on earth?"

Profoundly moved, I bowed and promised: "Father, I will be Thy faithful companion, loving and sincere, throughout Eternity. Shape me and make me worthy of my part in Thy cosmic Play and Thy Divine Mission."

44. The significance of a birthday

The soul comes down. Mother-Earth smiles. Father-Heaven smiles. Father smiles in His divine offering. Mother smiles in Her divine acceptance.

A soul comes not alone. It arrives with God's Promise and God's Fulfilment. A new Thought, a new Inspiration, a new Light, a new Power and a new Manifestation of God enter into a physical body, the fort of protection.

God once more inspires the soul and energises the body to enter dauntlessly into the battlefield of life with a stronger inspiration, a brighter freedom and a deeper peace.

Each birthday flowers into a special significance. The yet unfulfilled desires of a man knock at the Door of his soul. His soul opens the Door and comes to the fore on this special day.

The Supreme sends Eternity, Infinity and Immortality down into the world to feed His divine child, the soul. Eternity serves the breakfast, Infinity the lunch and Immortality the dinner. Eternity tells the soul where it is, Infinity tells the soul how far to go, Immortality tells the soul when and where to stop.

God dreams in the soul, for the soul. The soul dreams in the body, for the body. The body dreams in the senses, for the senses. The senses say to the body, the physical consciousness: "United we are playing our roles to fulfil you." The body then says to the soul: "I am coming to fulfil you. Please stay for a while."

The soul says to God: "I am come. Be pleased to fulfil Yourself in me."

45. Evolution

We know that there is some Being whom we call God. We know that there is something which we call the Soul. It was the great American philosopher, Emerson, who said: "God is an infinite circle whose centre is everywhere, but whose circumference is nowhere." We can say definitely that this centre is man's soul.

The soul is an eternal entity. Now what is its connection with reincarnation? One can write endless pages on reincarnation, that formidable concept which is so widely spoken about and just as widely disbelieved. Let us try to understand, in one short sentence, the essence of the matter. Reincarnation is the process by which the soul evolves; reincarnation exists for the growth and development of the soul.

We all know of Charles Darwin's theory of evolution, the evolution of species. It is the change in the physical organism from lower to higher, or from simpler to more complex. Spiritual evolution runs parallel to physical evolution. The soul exists in all beings. True, it is divine and immortal, but it has its own urge to be more complete, more fulfilling and more divine. Hence in the process of its evolution, it has to pass from the least perfect body to the most perfect body. Meanwhile it takes into itself the real value of all its earthly experiences. Thus the soul grows, enriching itself, making its divinity more integral, more harmonious and more perfect.

Reincarnation tells us that we have not come from nothing. Our present condition is the result of what we have made ourselves from our past. We are the consequence of our past incarnations.

"Many births have been left behind by Me and by thee, O Arjuna! All of them I know, but thou knowest not thine," said the Divine Krishna to the yet unrealised Arjuna.

Evolution is the hyphen between what was and what would be. I am a man. I must know that I was not only my father, but I shall also be my son. Problems I had. You had. He had. No exceptions. We faced them. We face them even today. But we shall solve them unmistakably.

We made a promise of transformation, a

promise that has no equal. We want the transformation of the inner and the outer. Each one of us may vision the face of transformation and finally be ourselves transformed. But how to achieve this transformation that will hold aloft the Torch of Immortality? For this we have to know what aspiration is and what doubt is.

Doubt is a destructive influence, an inner war, that works day and night to prey on our inner life. Aspiration, on the other hand, is the most effective energising power in a truth-seeker. It is at once the uplifting joy and the intensification of our consciousness. Aspiration places the thirst for Truth above and beyond all things.

Aspiration can be developed. It is like crossing a street, one step at a time. Each time we aspire, we perform in the very depth of our consciousness, a miracle of welcoming the Beyond. Aspiration is based on a spontaneous faith that visions the future. Aspiration comes from our faith in God; more so, our faith in ourselves. In the secrets of Aspiration, Reincarnation, Evolution and Transformation lie our true destiny, a Divine Immortality.

III — Indian devotional songs

46. *Invocation*

Agne naya supatha raye asman...

Agni! Lead us by the auspicious path to Prosperity;
Thou God who knowest all our deeds...

(From the *Rig Veda: I.189.1*)

A devotional song has a universal appeal. It appeals to the aspiring soul and elevates the consciousness. It appeals also to our hearts and minds. A devotional song expresses a universal spiritual emotion, a personal experience which rises like a flame towards God.

I wish to say a word about the Invocation I have just sung. The Vedas are the most ancient, the most inspiring and the most important of the Indian scriptures. The quintessence of the Vedic Truth is the concept of the Journey. This is the Journey of the Soul along the Path of Truth and Eternal Order. The Vedas overflow with love of life and energy for action; they invoke the Supreme with implicit faith for Guidance and Divine Inspiration.

The Vedas are four in number, each book containing several thousand hymns. The four Vedas are the Rig Veda, the Yajur Veda, the Sama Veda and the Atharva Veda. The hymn I have just sung is from the Rig Veda, from that part of it devoted to the adoration of Agni, the God of the Eternal Divine Fire. The "Prosperity" mentioned in the hymn is not merely earthly prosperity, but is an inner and all-fulfilling prosperity, a plenitude of both the Spirit and the outer life.

Now to come to the second song on the programme. The Upanishads are intuitive revelations derived from the Vedas. The Upanishads have inspired all systems of Indian philosophy and even today guide the spiritual lives of millions of Truth-seekers. God alone knows how many Upanishads once existed, but only 108 have been faithfully preserved. The Brihad-aranyaka Upanishad contains one of India's most significant and inspiring invocations to God. For centuries, the firmament of India has resounded with this beloved and immortal prayer:

Asato ma sad gamaya...

Lead us from the Unreal to the Real,
Lead us from Darkness unto Light,
Lead us from Death to Immortality.

(From the *Brihadaranyaka Upanishad*: I.3.28)

The Gita is the Song Celestial, sung by Lord Krishna himself. The Gita is the essence of all Indian scriptures. There are eighteen soul-illumining discourses in the Gita. In the eleventh one, Lord Krishna reveals to his beloved disciple, Arjuna, his Visva-Rupa, his Universal Form. On seeing this overpowering sight, this Divine Form, the surrendered disciple in Arjuna cries out:

Tvamadi Deva Purusha Purana...

Thou art the ancient Soul,
The first and original Godhead,
And the Supreme resting place of all that lives;
Thou art the Knower and the Known; the
   Highest Abode.
O Infinite in form, by Thee the Universe was extended.
Thou art Vayu and Yama and Agni and Soma
   and Varuna and Prajapati,
Father of creatures and the great-grandsire,
Salutation, Salutation to Thee,

A thousand times over and again,
And yet again, Salutation,
Again and again, Hail unto Thee.

(From the *Bhagavad-Gita: XI.38-39*)

In Vaishnavism, Sri Krishna is the sole object of love, devotion and worship. The Vaishnavites believe that unreserved dedication to Lord Krishna is the matchless ideal, the supreme way of life.

Radha, Lord Krishna's divine consort and disciple, is the very embodiment of that self-dedication. Having won Him by many lives of aspiration and devotion, she surrenders her very existence to serve Him.

Chandidas wrote this Bengali poem in the 16th century. He was a great Vaishnava poet, cherished by all in Bengal.

E ghora rajani meghera ghata...

The night is dark, the sky is filled with
    teeming clouds.
Friend, what can I say to you?
By virtue of many lives, Him I have won.

50

Rabindranath Tagore wrote:

> To the birds You gave songs,
> The birds gave You songs in return.
> You gave me only a voice,
> But You asked for more,
> And I sing.

Rabindranath was a Golden Song sung by the Divine Singer in him. He was, indeed, the World-Song, the golden chain that bound East and West.

He offered the world more than two thousand songs. He once said that when he was capable of singing, his own compositions were very few in number. But when he had become a prolific composer, his voice failed him and he was unable to sing most of his own songs.

He made a prophetic utterance about his own songs: "With the march of time, everything changes. But the Bengalees will sing my songs epoch after epoch. They will sing my songs in the hour of their sorrow, grief, joy and delight.

They will have no alternative."

In the song I shall now sing, Tagore compares the Pole-Star, fixed and steady in the dark night, with the light of the mind and heart which illumines the unlit existence of human life:

Nivid ghana andhare jwalichhe Dhruva tara...

In the tenebrous gloom shines the Pole-Star;
O my mind, in the immense expanse of night,
Lose not your Way.
Dead with depression and despair,
O my heart, cease not your singing.
Breaking asunder the prison of delusion,
Fulfil your life...

51

This is another song by Tagore.

Amar hiyar lukiye...

Lord, You have been hiding
In the inmost recesses of my heart.
I have not been able to see You.
To the world without, I have opened my eyes,
Not to the world within.
You were in all my loves and in all my pangs,
And in all my hopes;
You were beside me,
But I did not see You, I did not.

52

The next is an inspirational song written by Kaji Najrul Islam in the early decades of this century. It tells of the famous battle of Kurukshetra in the *Mahabharata*, addressing Lord Krishna, the Charioteer, and invoking Him to infuse man with courage and strength.

He Partha Sarathi, bajao, bajao Panchajanya...

O Charioteer,
Blow, blow your conch;
Drive away this depression of the heart.
Make them fearless who are struck with fear.
String the bow and hit the target.
Singing the mantra of the Gita,
Sacrifice your life.
Make us forget the fear of death.
Death is not the end of life.
Through Eternity flows the eternal tide of
  life...

53

I wrote the following song in India about fifteen years ago. It calls upon the soul to awaken and lead the entire being towards God-Realisation.

Jago amar swapan sathi, jago amar praner pran...

Awake, O Comrade of my dream,
Awake, O Breath of my life,
Awake, my Boundless Heart spread over the
 universe,
Awake, O that Consciousness of mine,
Which ends not,
Even crossing the Beyond.

Bande Mataram...

Mother, I bow to Thee...

This was the original national anthem of India, and the source of profound inspiration in the long struggle for India's independence.

The lines of the song were written by Bankim Chandra Chatterjee, the greatest novelist of Bengal and one of her men of supreme genius. The song appears in one of his greatest novels, *Ananda Math*.

No Indian will forget the role that this national song, *Bande Mataram*, played in the patriotic feeling of the Indian people. It served a Divine purpose in energising them in their long struggle for freedom. From the burning hearts of India's patriots, its flames of incantation rose high into the sky.

Many different tunes have been put to this song over the years. The present one was composed by a great musician of India, Dilip Kumar Roy.

Now we come to the last song, Phire Chalo.

By singing this song, a great singer of India, KC Dey, became immortal overnight. God had denied him sight; he was stone blind. But God sang through him in such soul-stirring grandeur as he performed this song for the famous film *Chandidasa* that his name became immortal in India.

In this song, Home is beckoning us. According to the Vedas, Home is Heaven on Earth, for it is by abiding in the soul here on earth that we achieve spiritual Bliss. In the Rig Veda, the seers sing: *Madhumat Punarayanam* which means "Sweet be my return [home]."

Phire Chalo, apana Ghare...

Let us return Home, let us go back,
Useless is this reckoning of seeking and getting,
...
Delight permeates all of today.
From the blue ocean of death

Life is flowing like nectar.
In life there is death; in death there is life.
So where is fear, where is fear?
The birds in the sky are singing
　"No death, no death!"
Day and night the tide of Immortality
Is descending here on earth.

IV — Essays, part 2

56. *A spiritual giant and a seer-poet*

Vivekananda was a flaming tongue of fire. Tagore was a sea of beauty and delight. Vivekananda was a clarion-call. Tagore was a soul-stirring flute. To both, humanity was a great love, dynamic and powerful on the part of Vivekananda, soft and sweet on the part of Tagore.

Vivekananda says in effect: "No time to linger! Awake, O India and with your dauntless strength, achieve the loftiest height of your Spirit." Tagore says in effect: "Look everywhere and see God's beauty, and then, O Ind, raise your proud head towards the Highest."

With his spirit's height, Vivekananda was the most nourishing, life-giving fruit. With his creative genius, Rabindranath was the most beautiful flower. The Goddess Mahakali shone in the eyes of Vivekananda. The Goddess Mahalakshmi smiled through the eyes of

Rabindranath.

Yet it was only after the recognition of the West that the East would claim them, the spiritual giant by the impact of his Chicago address, the mystic poet by virtue of his *Gitanjali*.

In both cases, the divine singer expressed himself in divine measure. Through his spiritual emotion and his soul-stirring voice, Narendra pleased his divine Master, Ramakrishna, and through him, the world. By his soul-awakening songs of transcendental beauty, Rabindranath charmed the world and seized the All-Blissful.

Both Narendranath and Rabindranath came into the world from the Unknown. They were, as it were, two tireless voyagers. Rabindranath touched the earth-sphere in 1861, just two fleeting years before Narendranath. Narendranath left earth and entered the upper-sphere in 1902, thirty-nine long years before Rabindranath.

Verily, Vivekananda and Tagore were pilgrims to Infinity's Shore, where the finite, at last, has its perfect Play.

57. Vivekananda speaks about Christ

> These great children of Light, who manifest the light themselves, they, being worshipped, become as it were, one with us and we have become one with them.

– Vivekananda

It is easier to have faith in the Personal God than in the Impersonal. God dons the earthly cloak. He bodies forth the creation of his own time and casts a far-flung glance into the yet unborn to bring it into existence. He reveals Himself to each individual according to his power of receptivity.

To the beginner, Christ would immediately speak of the Personal God. "Pray to your Father in Heaven." To the one a little more advanced, he would say, "I am the vine, ye are the branches." But to the one who is fully advanced and his dear disciple, he would proclaim: "I and my Father are One." We find the same truth echoed in Sri Ramakrishna's words. He disclosed to his beloved Naren (Vivekananda), "He who is Rama, He who is Krishna, dwells at once in this body as Ramakrishna."

It is a sad fact that often the disciples of various paths misinterpret the teachings of their Masters to the extent of claiming theirs as the only Master. In doing so, they bring their teachers down to the level of an ordinary man. An aspirant, they claim, in spite of high achievements, counts for nothing unless and until he is prepared to give all credit to their particular Master. What blind ignorance! If the Master were an ear-witness of his disciples' utterance, he would be burned with shame. On this Vivekananda says:

> Suppose Jesus of Nazareth was teaching, and a man came and told him, "What you teach is beautiful. I believe that it is the way to perfection, and I am ready to follow it; but I do not want to worship you as the only begotten Son of God." What would be the answer of Jesus of

Nazareth?

"Very well, brother, follow the ideal and advance in your own way. I do not care whether you give me the credit for the teaching or not... I only teach truth, and truth is nobody's property, nobody's patent truth. Truth is God Himself. Go forward." But what the disciples say nowadays is, "No matter whether you practise the teachings or not, do you give credit to the Man? If you credit the Master, you will be saved; if not there is no salvation for you."

An interesting anecdote took place when Vivekananda was staying at the Thousand Island Park. It was a dark and rainy night. A few ladies from Detroit had travelled hundreds of miles to find him there. Having met him, one of them humbly spoke out, "We have come to you just as we would go to Jesus if he were still on the earth and ask him to teach us." Vivekananda, deeply moved and overwhelmed with humility, replied, "If only I possessed the power of Christ to set you free now!"

Christ unveiled the truth, "The Kingdom of Heaven is within you." A heroic echo is heard in Vivekananda: "It is already yours... It is yours by right." We are drawn to the famous lines of the Gita: "He who seeth Me everywhere and seeth everything in Me, of him will I never lose hold, nor shall he ever lose hold of Me." Almost parallel to this, are the divine words of Christ: "He that loseth his life for my sake shall find it."

The Nazarene was a product of the East, although the people of the West have managed to forget this bare truth. "An Oriental of Orientals," said Vivekananda of the son of Mary. It is quite natural that in the Bible we come across many images, symbols, natural scenes and simple ways of living common to the oriental countries. But what is more important; the oriental view is that this material life falls short of true satisfaction. So when Christ says: "Not this life, but something higher," Vivekananda cannot help remarking, "Like a true son of the

Orient, he is practical in that."

Vivekananda meant that our earthly achievements, however grandiose, are in no way enough to quench the ever-pinching thirst of human souls to attain to a higher life.

Christ's body is Christianity. Christianity embodies humility. Vivekananda's humility the entire world treasures. He once said:

> If you ask me, "Is there a God?" and I say, "Yes," you immediately ask my grounds for saying so, and poor me has to exercise all his powers to provide you with some reason. If you had come to Christ and said, "Is there any God?" he would have said, "Yes," and if you had asked, "Is there any proof?" he would have replied, "Behold the Lord."

58. Vivekananda and America

He who broke the barrier between East and West and placed the two on common ground is still a living force in both. His function was to bring in oneness where there was none before, by carrying the best of each to the other. The East had become lost by moving away from materialism; the West by keeping clear of spirituality. A happy marriage of the two, he deeply felt, was the supreme need of the world. Life without spirituality was as poor as life without material power. Hence he dynamised the East with the force of the West, and inspired the West with the ancient wisdom of the East.

It is foolish to think that he sailed for America to satisfy his mental curiosity. It is also an absurdity to believe that his feet touched foreign shores to make a noise in the world. No. It was Sri Ramakrishna's silent blessing that kindled the inspiration-fire of the beloved disciple to share his light with the soil and soul of America.

No country is superior to others in all spheres of life. Vivekananda with his deeply penetrating insight says: "As regards spirituality, the Americans are far inferior to us, but their society is far superior to ours." He showed how a happy and true union could be effected between the other-world-loving Indians and the this-world-loving Americans: "We will teach them our spirituality and assimilate what is best in their society."

Asia, Europe and America – each continent made a contribution of its own to the world at large. With the help of his spirit's vision, Vivekananda revealed the truth: "Asia laid the germs of civilisation, Europe developed man, and America is developing woman and the masses."

It is an established fact that the women in America are the most advanced in the world, especially in the cultivation of knowledge. Vivekananda made a surprising observation: "The average American woman is far more cultivated than the average American man." He further added: "The men slave all their life for money and the women snatch every opportunity to improve themselves." His highest compliment to women came when he said: "I have seen thousands of women here whose hearts are as pure and stainless as snow." And again: "American women! A hundred lives would not be sufficient to pay my deep debt of gratitude to you! I have not words enough to express my gratitude to you."

However, he was also deeply indebted to American men. For it was JH Wright, Professor of Greek at Harvard University, who was first in realising what Vivekananda was. It was when the Indian monk was found, prior to his becoming a delegate to the Parliament of Religions, to be almost destitute, no better than a street-beggar. Verily, Professor Wright, that blessed son of America, was a man of action. He introduced Vivekananda to the President of the "Parliament" in Chicago. The Professor's flaming and instructive words have echoed and re-echoed in the hearts of both East and West: "To ask you, Swami, for your credentials is like asking the Sun to state its right to shine."

Vivekananda's soul-stirring addresses inspired the audience to have faith in all the religions of the world, to hug the best in each religion. There was a magic spell of throbbing delight woven around his very name at the

Parliament of Religions. He was the figure that dominated the world's gaze there. A report appeared in the *Boston Evening Transcript* of 30 September 1893 about the great triumph of the Indian spiritual giant: "If he merely crosses the Platform, he is applauded, and this marked approval of thousands he accepts in a child-like spirit of gratification, without a trace of conceit."

The same paper on 5 April 1894 had an irresistible recollection:

> At the Parliament of Religions, they used to keep Vivekananda until the end of the programme, to make people stay until the end of the session. On a warm day, when a prosy speaker talked too long and people began going home by hundreds, the Chairman would get up and announce that Swami Vivekananda would make a short address just before the benediction. Then he would have the peaceful hun-

dreds perfectly in tether. The four thousand fanning people in the Hall of Columbus would sit smiling and expectant, waiting for an hour or two of other men's speeches, to listen to Vivekananda for fifteen minutes.

In no time, America realised that Vivekananda was no isolated dreamer, nor, unlike most spiritual figures of the East, did he care primarily for his own personal salvation. They discovered in him a lofty spiritual realist and a universal lover of humanity. It was his vast personality and his spiritual inspiration that achieved for him such acclaim in America. Vivekananda's credo was characterised by its freedom; thus the freedom-loving Americans responded enthusiastically to his message. They accepted his teaching that material prosperity and spiritual aspiration must run abreast and help each other if man is to see the full face of Divine Knowledge.

It is indeed only when we live in this truth

that we can bask in the glorious Sunshine of the Soul that is Vivekananda.

59. America in her depths

"Of what use to me are the things that cannot make me immortal?"

Thus in her longing for Immortality, the great woman of the Upanishads, Maitreyi, rejects the riches of the world. By Immortality, she does not mean the continuity of her human existence, but a life to be lived in her soul.

India's history is aglow with kings and potentates enjoying power and opulence without being in the least attached to them. Rajarshi Janaka was not an isolated instance. Prince Siddhartha, afterwards Buddha, and Emperor Asoka are other such outstanding figures in history.

Of all the nations in the world today, America is the one which, in the modern context, stands forth uniquely as the most fit for the ideal of Janaka, Siddhartha and Asoka. By the flow of her wealth, America has restored shattered Europe, not once but twice. Impoverished India has been helped towards her goal of achieving minimum conditions of life for her vast millions through large-scale and repeated American aid.

Many other countries, large and small, have shared in America's munificence. Not only her generosity, but her ever-progressive mind and the dynamism of her spirit have been an asset to the whole international community.

In a little over a century after achieving her Independence, America accepted into her wide-open heart a wandering young Sannyasi's message. The fact that Swami Vivekananda's message of the pervasive oneness and unity of all creation was appreciated and understood at the Parliament of Religions held in Chicago in 1893, shows the character of America's evolving progressive spirit.

This very spirit, being the essence of her national Self, is bound to transcend its present limits and soar into the heights of spiritual oneness. Indications are already available in the works of her advanced thinkers of the growth of her mind towards the summit of her evolution, a summit manifesting the successful spiritual transformation of her life and thought. Who knows that she will not be the first to respond to the call of God, to the unique task of self-transmutation into the consciousness of the Soul? If in a post-war world, she has been a great helper, what role will be hers in the world of tomorrow, when God's Voice will be heard through all human lips?

Until now, the world has seen largely the surfaces of American life, and it has formed its opinion accordingly. Not that her depths have not occasionally come to view, but such occasions have been few in relation to the vastness and variety of her population. Needless to say, there are great indications of a greater future, and as the Hour of God dawns and advances towards its fullness, the splendour of America's soul will show more and more on the surface, even for crude eyes to see.

Every nation has its soul. The soul of a nation consists in its aspirations, aptitudes and capacities placed at the service of the Supreme. Now that a spiritual awakening is upon the world, it is only a question of years (and certainly not centuries) before its golden glint falls on the face of every nation. The Divinity now hidden beneath the surface will shine forth, to a greater or lesser degree, upon each one.

Judging from her history, America holds out the brightest promise of placing at the Service of the Divine her aspirations, aptitudes and capacities, as she has often, in times of need, placed them at the service of humanity.

Furthermore, it is not only for political and economic purposes that the divine logic of events has brought India and America close together. What is seen in these external aspects of life will be seen in an incalculable measure on the deeper levels in days to come. America is, perhaps, not conscious that in taking a major part in the economic rehabilitation of India, she has been building up the base of a divine new world. And if America is doing so much for the base, she cannot but do much more for the superstructure. Then will prosperous America be doubly prosperous, spiritual prosperity being added to the material, and both nourishing and serving the highest cause of a Divine New Creation.

60. Beauty

An unaspiring man desires beauty without. A seeker of Peace desires beauty within. A lover of God desires both beauty within and beauty without.

The outer beauty sought for by a lover of God is totally different from the beauty cried for by an unaspiring man. An unaspiring man is both tempted and tempting. When he is tempted, he wants the outer world of beauty to cherish him. When he is tempting, he wants to bind the outer world of beauty. His acts of tempting others and of being tempted by others eventually lead him into frustration. Lo, inside his frustration there are two animals, a tiger and a cat. The cat is being devoured by the tiger. Soon he comes to realise that the tiger is none other than his all-devouring ego, and that the cat is none other than his ever-crying and begging desire.

A God-lover's outer beauty: he wants his outer beauty to inspire the length and breadth of the world. His beauty is the beauty of a fragrant rose. His beauty is the affection of an affectionate mother. His beauty is the beauty of a fruitful tree.

A fragrant rose makes our outer body fragrant. An affectionate mother offers to our outer life a flood of affection. A fruitful tree reminds us of our inner tree which bears joy, countless joys.

A God-lover's inner beauty: it is the flowering of his consciousness. His inner beauty is the height of his aspiration. His inner beauty is the light of his realisation.

The outer beauty is the necessity of humanity. The inner beauty is the light of his divinity.

An aspirant is really beautiful when he comes to learn that he is all heart. An aspirant is divinely beautiful when he feels that he is all soul. An aspirant is supremely beautiful when he discovers that he has in abundant measure what God eternally is.

When we live in the emotional vital, our beauty is an outer gift. When we live in the aspiring heart, our beauty is an inner gift. The outer gift feels the outer world as a world of strangers. The inner gift feels the inner world as a world of illumining and illumined oneness.

*

Beauty without light is a flower without fragrance. Beauty with light is a human flower full of fragrance and without ignorance.

The beauty of life is our purity's spontaneity. The beauty of truth is our sincerity's necessity. The beauty of God-Realisation is our aspiration's divinity.

We look beautiful within when our passions die. We look more beautiful within when our inner flame mounts. We look most beautiful within when our sun of realisation bursts.

The power of beauty is an aspirant's manifested motherhood. The peace of beauty is an aspirant's fulfilled fatherhood. The bliss of beauty is an aspirant's transformed and divinised manhood and womanhood.

When I am physically beautiful, God smiles. God smiles at me because I am using His own dress. When I am spiritually beautiful, God plays. God plays with me because He has got me as His own playmate.

He who does not spiritually become the pages of cosmic beauty will one day ruthlessly be compelled to read the Book of Fate, by Ignorance. Not even God, the Compassionate, will hide the Book of Fate from him.

If we start with the soul's beauty, we can end in the Supreme's transcendental Reality. Let us start

*

Obscurity says to Beauty: "Beauty, why are you so beautiful?"

Beauty answers, "Obscurity, better ask me how I am so beautiful and not why. I am beautiful because I always touch the Feet of God with my heart's soulful cry."

Purity speaks to Beauty: "Beauty, I wish to stay with you for some time."

Beauty answers, "Purity, certainly you may. I would love to have you. But don't forget to bring your identification."

"What *is* my identification?" asks Purity.

"Don't you know what your identification is? Your identification is your life-long spontaneity."

Austerity speaks to Beauty: "Beauty, you are a fool. You never aspire. I am really sorry to tell you that you are God's only failure."

"Austerity, granted, I am God's failure. But certainly you are no better than I am. Remember, God is all Love. Remember, God is all Sweetness."

Calamity says to Beauty: "Beauty, I loved you. Look at my deplorable consciousness. Look at Time which has deserted me. Look at my fallen life!"

"Calamity, I can solve all your problems, once and for all. Give me your deplorable consciousness. From now on, it will live with my inner life. Give me Time that has deserted you. From now on, it will live with my inner breath. Give me your fallen life. From now on, it will live with my inner Goal."

Dignity speaks to Beauty: "Beauty, I understand perfectly why others bow down to you, but I do not know what makes me bow to you."

"Dignity, your heart's necessity tells you that I have the power to increase your nobility's light and your honour's height."

Hostility says: "Beauty, my name is Hostility. I want to destroy you. I want to banish you from

God's World. I want to destroy your beauty, both inner and outer, here and now."

Beauty says, "Hostility, you can never destroy me because God the Necessity is immortalising me from within. God the Omnipotent Reality is protecting me, cherishing me and fulfilling me from without."

Divinity whispers: "Can you tell me, Beauty, why I need you throughout Eternity?"

"Mother, you need me because within me you see your own everlasting divine sovereignty."

61. God the supreme Musician

God, the Musician, knows that music is Spirituality, music is Immortality. Man, the musician, thinks that music is sensuality, music is mortality.

God, the Musician, knows that His music is His Transcendental Self-Communion. Man, the musician, feels only that his music is his world's life-long companion.

God, the Musician, is divinely and eternally Mysterious. Man, the musician, is humanly and temporarily marvellous.

God's music tells us that music is the realisation of the universal soul. Man's music tells us that music is the aspiration of the individual soul.

God's music starts at the Height and runs to the Depth. Man's music starts at the breadth and runs to the length. On the Height, God's music is His vision. In the Depth, God's music is His Reality. In the breadth, man's music is his crying soul. In the length, man's music is his victory's goal.

God's music is the constant expansion of His

soul's delight. Man's music is the preparation of his life's hunger for perpetual joy.

God's music inundates God with its infinite luminosity. Man's music inundates man with its endless curiosity.

Music in the unlit body is destruction. Music in the unlit vital is passion. Music in the unlit mind is confusion. Music in the unlit heart is frustration.

Music in the aspiring body is creation. Music in the aspiring vital is purification. Music in the aspiring mind is liberation. Music in the aspiring heart is revelation.

My God, the Supreme Musician, has two families. One is in the East, the other in the West. He tells His Eastern children, precisely His Indian children, that music is the soul's purity. He tells His Western children that music is life's beauty.

He tells His Eastern children that music is the fulfilling rest at the bottom of the life-sea. He tells His Western children that music is the dance of the multitudinous waves of the life-sea.

He tells His Eastern children, "My children, among you, those who can run will run; those who can march will march; and those who can walk will walk towards their Destined Goal." He tells His Western children, "My children, I want you all to stay together. I want you all to run together towards your Destined Goal." He tells His Eastern children, "My children, what you have is a one-pointed and unbroken chain of unity. That is good." He tells His Western children, "My children, what you have is unity in diversity. That is great."

He tells His Eastern children, "My children, what you have is your dream's poetry; what you have is your reality's literature."

He tells His Western children, "My children, what you have is your reality's mathematics, what you have is your dream's architecture."

Here we are all seekers, seekers of the Infinite Truth. I wish to tell you that Beethoven was also a genuine seeker. Some of you are consumed with the desire to arouse and awaken your *Kundalini*, so that you can have occult powers to perform miracles. Well, I wish to tell you that you do not have to practise any specific spiritual discipline in order to awaken your Kundalini.

Beethoven is a striking example of how one's own soulful music, inspired by the higher worlds, can awaken the Kundalini. His music did this very thing for him and awakened that serpent force. The Kundalini, that dormant power lying latent at the base of the spine, arose from its slumbers through the force of Beethoven's soulful creations. It forced its way upward into the higher chakras of his body and found its glorious release in the magnificent power and immensity of his later symphonies. You may try with your own soul's music. You are not Beethoven, but I assure you that you, too, will succeed.

Now what Beethoven says about music is true, not only from the intellectual and emotional point of view, but also from the spiritual point of view.

> "Music is the mediator between the spiritual and the sensual life. Although the spirit be not master of that which it creates through music, yet it is blessed in this crea-

tion, which, like every creation of
art, is mightier than the artist."

Music is the Vedic bird in us. This bird divine, called Suparna, flies in the welkin of Infinity, through Eternity, with the message of Immortality. Here on earth, we do notice that the birds have the capacity to sing in endless measure, whereas we human beings are bound to our very few creations. Tagore sings with us:

> To the birds You gave songs,
> The birds gave You songs in return.
> You gave me only a voice,
> But You asked for more,
> And I sing.

The poet-bird in Keats, divinely intoxcated, flies in front of me, before my ken.

> Was it a vision, or a waking dream?
> Fled is that music: – Do I wake or
>   sleep?

The music-bird is within, to stay, to give us love.

The music-bird is without, to fly, to give us joy.

Since music is a universal language, it has no need to express itself in any particular language of the world. Rabindranath Tagore says, "Music is the purest form of art, and, therefore, the most direct expression of beauty, with a form and spirit which is one and simple, and least encumbered with anything extraneous. We seem to feel that the manifestation of the infinite in the finite forms of creation is music itself, silent and visible."

Our body's food is the product of the earth: fruits and vegetables and so forth. But our soul's food is music. Undoubtedly it is so. Even our physical nature at times intensely craves and desperately needs music.

What Bouvée says is undeniably true. "Music is the fourth great material want of our nature – first food, then raiment, then shelter, then music."

In the spiritual world, next to meditation comes music, the breath of music. Meditation is silence, energising and fulfilling. Silence is the eloquent expression of the inexpressible. "After silence, that which comes nearest to expressing the inexpressible is music."

Someone said, "Music is another woman who talks charmingly, but says nothing." I say, "Music is verily the woman who, at once, says everything divinely and offers her soul unreservedly."

They say, "Classical music is the music without words; modern music is the music without music." I say, "Classical music is the music that lasts after it has all been played; modern music is the music that begins long before it actually begins." In classical music we try to see God the Eternal Beyond. In modern music we see God the Eternal Now.

Music is our soul's home. God is the Supreme Musician. His Flute stirs the universal consciousness. He plays on His Flute. We listen. We do something more. We barter our body's dust with His Soul's plenitude.

To God, the Supreme Musician, we bow.

62

Man is Infinity's Heart
Man is Eternity's Breath
Man is Immortality's Life

APPENDIX

BIBLIOGRAPHY

Sri Chinmoy:

Eternity's Breath, Sri Chinmoy Lighthouse, New York, 1972.

Suggested citation key is: ETB

Table of Contents

Eternity's Breath   9
Appendix   89
Bibliography   91
Table of Contents   93

The heart-traveller

1. Aspiration-Flames — Aspiration and God's Hour
2. A Sri Chinmoy primer
3. Everest-Aspiration
4. New Year's Messages from Sri Chinmoy (1966-2007)
5. Flower-Flames
6. Songs of the Soul
7. Eternity's Breath

www.ingramcontent.com/pod-product-compliance
Lightning Source LLC
Chambersburg PA
CBHW030301100526
44590CB00012B/481